How to make hand hooked
RAG RUGS

ANN DAVIES

SEARCH PRESS

First published in Great Britain 1996

Search Press Limited
Wellwood, North Farm Road,
Tunbridge Wells, Kent TN2 3DR

ISBN 0 85532 807 X

Suppliers
If you have any difficulty in obtaining any of
the materials and equipment mentioned in this
book, then please write for a current list of
stockists, including firms who operate a mail-
order service, to the Publishers.

Search Press Limited, Wellwood,
North Farm Road, Tunbridge Wells,
Kent TN2 3DR, England.

The author would like to thank P&Q, of Bishop's
Frome, Worcester, who provided the stencils used
for the director's chair on page 36 and the seat pad
on page 37, and Roma Kirke for some of the designs
used in this book.

Printed in Spain by Elkar S. Coop, Bilbao 48012

*For my late husband, Neil, who was always so
supportive of my work.*

Front cover
STAINED-GLASS CIRCLES
Designed by Ann Davies

*I am very fond of stained-glass effects, and I based this
design on various medieval stained glass found in
cathedrals throughout Europe. The materials are all
different kinds of velvet – cotton velvet, panné velvet
and stretch imitation velvet, When using stretch
fabrics, always cut strips slightly wider than normal.
Size: 810mm (32in) diameter*

Page 1
RADIATING SQUARES *(See page 39)*

Contents

£5·95

Introduction

Making rag rugs is an enjoyable, inexpensive pastime which requires a minimum outlay on tools and basic equipment. It is a traditional craft which has gone through varying periods of popularity and almost total oblivion.

In the late-nineteenth and early-twentieth centuries it was associated with poverty, and was often the only way working-class people could afford to have a rug (popularly called a 'mat') on their cold floors. As people became more affluent they did not want to admit to having rag mats, but there were always areas of the British Isles where the craft was kept alive.

During the Second World War the 'Make-do and mend' campaign encouraged people to recycle their clothes and other fabrics, and rag rugs became fashionable again. This was short lived and, after the war, it again became something of a forgotten craft.

However, there is now a growing perception of the need to conserve and recycle materials, and interest in the various aspects of rag-rug making has revived. Awareness of rag-rug making as a textile art, and as a craft is on the increase. Some of the leading textile designers, both in Britain and North America, are now becoming conscious of rag-rug making.

It is a craft which has universal appeal. Anyone can make a rag rug, and the craft can be adapted to a variety of other articles – wallhangings, cushions, tea cosies, chair pads, mirror surrounds, table mats – the list is endless.

Discarded clothing has been a traditional source for rag-rug making for a great many years. In Scandinavia rags were, and still are, woven into floor and bed coverings. In Britain it was quite an occasion when a new rug was finished – often all the family had been involved in its making – and it was laid before the fire in the living room. (Sometimes, before being used on the floor, the new rug was put on the bed for warmth.) The rug that had been in the living room was removed to the scullery, and the rug from there was placed in the outside lavatory or, sometimes, in the dog kennel! The oldest rug was then thrown away. Not all this heritage was destroyed, however, and examples of rag rugs can be seen in various folk museums around the country, but it was usually the better designed and more colourful ones that were kept.

My own introduction to rag-rug making came in the mid nineteen-sixties when I was studying embroidery at college. Embroidery was at an exciting stage and students were encouraged to investigate and experiment with a wide variety of threads and materials. At that time I was only aware of the hooked rag rugs made in North America (there was very little written history or information about rag-rug making in Britain). After incorporating embroidery with rag-rug techniques, I became more and more interested in the various aspects of rag-rug making and, despite knowing many techniques, I have to admit that I love the texture and effect of hooked rag rugs.

Hooked rag rugs produce a looped effect, in contrast to the shaggy look often associated with traditional rag rugs.

I hope that you too will find this an all-absorbing interest. Relax; have fun. I always warn my students that rag-rug making should carry a Government health warning. If you are not careful, it can become very addictive!

Opposite
WISE OLD OWL
Designed by Roma Kirke

This subject, which I believe is based on a horned owl, is everyone's favourite, but it is not a beginner's piece! Tweedy woollen materials were used for the feathers.
Size: 560 x 735mm (22 x 29in)

Basic equipment and fabrics

The equipment used to make rag rugs is relatively simple and inexpensive. The frame and hook are probably the most expensive pieces, but, once you have purchased them, you will never have to buy them again. The picture opposite illustrates these items together with the other tools you need. Usually, the base fabric is hessian (burlap). Linen is becoming more widely used, but this can be very expensive. However, you can use any even-weave fabric through which you can easily push the hook.

Of course, you will also need lots of materials to hook with, and I discuss these on pages 9–10.

Hook

Hooks have a tapered shank (usually made of brass) set in a wooden handle. The taper allows the tool to make different sizes of holes in the base fabric so that various thicknesses of material can be used. The actual hook at the pointed end of the shank is set at an acute angle.

Around the world there are various sizes of hook available but, for all the rugs in this book I used a standard (primitive) size, which can be used with various thicknesses of fabrics. If you want to work with knitting wools and fine-cut materials you will need a finer hook.

These hooks can only be purchased from specialist suppliers. The average craft shop will usually offer a latch hook, which is totally unsuitable.

Frame

A frame is essential. When you are starting out, artists' stretchers will be fine. They are mitred at each corner and slot together. You can buy them in art shops and they come in a variety of lengths. Alternatively, you can use four flat pieces of wood joined firmly together at the corners.

The largest rug you can make using a fixed frame is about 710mm (28in) wide. This is because you work with one arm under the frame and one on top. If you use too large a frame, you will find it difficult to hook properly.

You can make a larger rug in a number of ways. The simplest method is to work on small sections and then join them together, but this does create weak areas in the rug. You can also join work by overlapping the base fabric and hooking through the two layers. This should be done off the frame and is not easy, but it does overcome the problem of weak areas. Alternatively, stretch part of a large piece of base fabric on the frame, hook that area, remove it and then stretch and hook another part.

In North America rug makers use various kinds of lap frame, or sometimes they use a large quilting frame.

You can buy special frames on which you wind long lengths of base fabric. However, these are expensive so I suggest you start with a cheap frame and then, when you get addicted, you can invest in more sophisticated frames.

Whatever frame you use, it should always be at least 50mm (2in) bigger all round than the intended finished piece so, for a 600mm (24in) width you need a 650mm (26in) frame.

Base fabric – hessian (burlap)

Choose good quality fabric – your time is too valuable to waste on second-class materials. I use a fine 340g (12oz) hessian which has not been coated with an inflammable finish; it is available in widths up to 1.8m (72in). Fabrics bought from an upholstery supplier will normally be flame resistant, but this type of finish makes it difficult to push the hook through the threads.

The piece of fabric must fit the frame to its outside edge. If you wish to work on a large piece, join small pieces as described above.

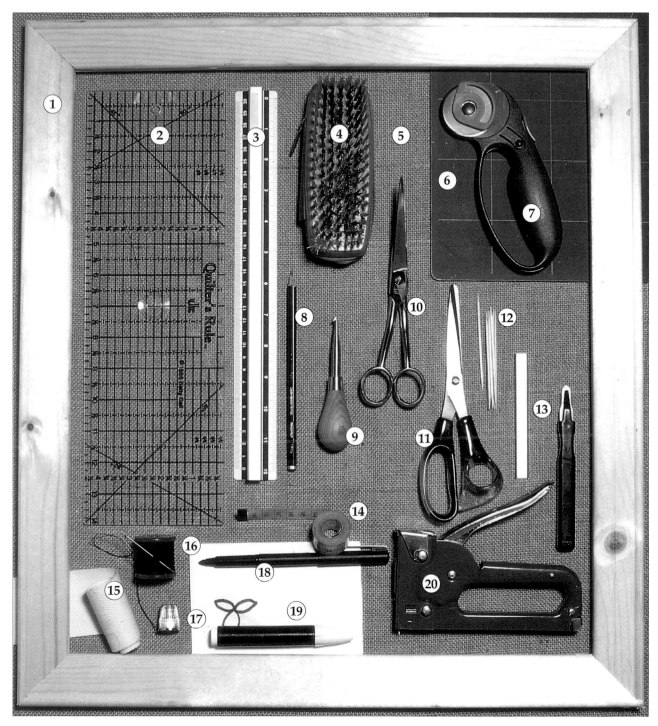

1. Frame made with artist's stretchers
2. Quilter's rule
3. Ruler
4. Clothes brush
5. Base fabric – hessian (burlap)
6. Cutting mat
7. Rotary cutter
8. HB pencil
9. Hook
10. Napping scissors
11. Cutting out scissors
12. Cocktail sticks
13. Staples and remover
14. Tape measure
15. Carpet braid
16. Sewing thread and needle
17. Thimble
18. Waterproof felt-tipped pen
19. Transfer pen and paper
20. Staple gun

Other tools and materials

Hooked rugs are made using narrow strips of fabric which must be cut on the straight, never on the bias, using a sharp pair of dressmaking **scissors**. Alternatively, you can use a **rotary cutter** and a **self-healing mat**. There are also machines for cutting strips in various widths using different cutting wheels.

Use an **HB pencil** with a good point for outlining the borders and centre of your rug (see page 14).

A **ruler** and/or a **tape measure** is used to size the base fabric and to measure borders. My workbox also includes a **quilter's rule**.

You need a medium point, waterproof, **felt-tipped pen** to mark out your design on to the base fabric. If the design is simple, draw it directly on to the fabric after you have stretched it. If it is complicated, it is helpful to put the design on to the fabric before stretching it on to the frame.

A **transfer pen** (and transfer paper) will help you trace a design on to the fabric (see page 25).

The base fabric must be stretched and fixed firmly on to the frame. Best results are achieved using a **staple gun**, but you can use **drawing pins** (thumb tacks). A **staple remover** is a useful addition to the workbox.

Wooden **cocktail sticks** are useful for marking unhooked areas that are only visible on the back of the rug (see page 20).

Carpet braid, strong sewing **thread**, a **needle** and a **thimble** are needed to bind the edges of a rug. I use carpet binding (a twill weave tape) which is available in various colours and widths. I try to get a binding which blends in with the last row of hooking; otherwise I buy cream or neutral and dye it to the colour I want. This tape can shrink by up to 50mm per metre (2in per yard) so buy enough to go all around the rug, plus an allowance for the corners, some for shrinkage, and a little extra to turn under and butt the raw ends. Wash the tape and iron it flat.

Finally, on completion of the work, a firm **clothes brush** will prove useful to remove all the loose fibres.

You can hook with a wide selection of materials.

Hooking materials

A wide variety of fabrics can be used in rag-rug making. The original fabrics used were natural fibres, mainly woollen, but nowadays we have a considerable range of fabrics available in our rag bag. Thrift is still the order of the day and woollens, jersey, felted jumpers and cardigans, blankets (preferably wool or with a high-wool content), flannclette sheets, synthetics such as viscose, velvets and stretch fabrics are just some of the materials that can be used.

Cotton can be used, but bear in mind that it flattens easily and has no natural resilience; in other words, it does not spring back when trodden on. The Amish in the United States have produced some wonderful rugs in which cotton has been used and, over the years, the loops have been flattened, giving the appearance of mosaic.

I use a lot of woollen material, including old blankets. I find woollen fabric very satisfying, and it dyes wonderfully (see pages 26–27). Yarns can be used but they must not be too thin, unless you use a very fine hook. You can also hook with lots of other materials (see pages 10–11)

Always wash your materials before you use them. This not only enables you to see whether the colour runs, but also ensures that the material is clean and thus less likely to attract moths. If you are using old clothing, take the garment to pieces by unpicking the seams and discard zips, buttons and worn areas before washing.

If your material is one that frays, place it in a net laundry bag before putting it in the washing machine. This will ensure that the loose fibres do not clog the washing machine. If you have a loose woollen material you can also, by using a high-temperature hot-wash cycle, sometimes felt the material, making it easier to hook with.

Always cut your fabrics on the straight of the material, never on the bias.

How much material will cover a given area? This depends on the height of the loops and the width of the strips. As a general guide, fold a piece of material four times and place it on your base fabric; the area that the folded material covers will be roughly the same size as you will be able to hook.

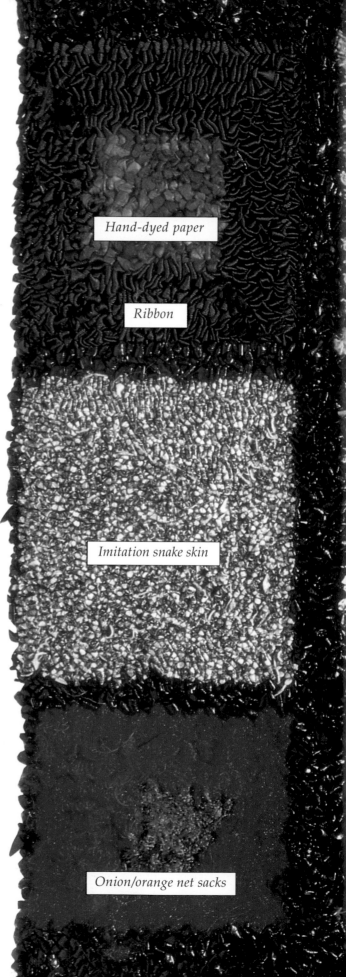

Hand-dyed paper

Ribbon

Imitation snake skin

Onion/orange net sacks

When making less practical items such as wallhangings, mirror surrounds, etc., investigate the possibilities of using other materials – leather, plastic bags, bin liners, reusable paper kitchen cloths, towelling, orange bags, unspun wool, knitting wools, crisp and sweet bags, raffia – the list is endless. The surround and intersections on the sampler opposite are made of strips cut from a black plastic sack; the panels were hooked with a number of other unusual materials.

Towelling

Leather

Crisp (chip) bags

Plastic carrier bags

Unspun carded fleece

Reusable paper kitchen cloths

Hooking a rug

The design

In this chapter I will take you through all the stages of making a rectangular rug using a tongue-and-mouth jigsaw design. This simple design came about because I was given a large bunch of tailor's swatches in black and white mixtures. It also provided an opportunity to use up relatively small pieces of materials left over from other projects.

The structure of a jigsaw is quite random and you do not need to have a formal pattern to copy.

For this exercise I simply drew some jigsaw pieces on to a piece of paper, using the tongue-and-mouth shapes to make a fully interlocking design. I also tried to maintain a uniform width and depth of each piece to give vertical columns and horizontal rows.

You need a frame measuring 650 x 910mm (26 x 36in), a piece of base fabric and a selection of different coloured fabrics.

Part of the paper pattern for the jigsaw puzzle design.

Framing the base fabric

1 First set up the frame. If you use artists'
stretchers they will already be mitred at the
corners, and are simply pushed together. At first,
the corners can be difficult to fit together. If this is
the case, use a rubber hammer, or a piece of firm
wood, to gently knock the corners together.

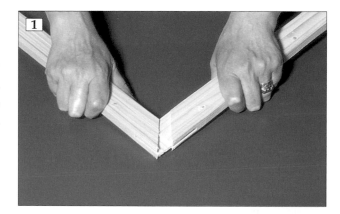

2 Now prepare the base fabric. Measure out
what you require, remembering that it must
fit to the outside edge of the frame. Pull out
threads to ensure you cut the fabric on the straight.

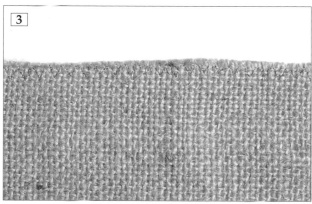

3 To prevent fraying while you work, sew zig-
zag stitches around the edges of the base
fabric, either with a sewing machine or by hand.

> **Tip**
> If you have a complicated design, draw the
> design on to the base fabric before you fix it to
> the frame.

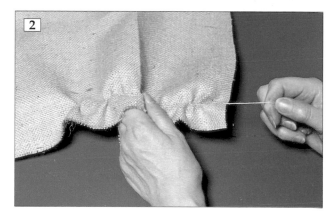

4 Now, start to fix the base fabric on to the
frame using either a staple gun or drawing
pins. Start by fixing one of the long straight edges
of the fabric along one of the long straight edges
of the frame. Be generous with your staples or
drawing pins. Then fix one of the adjacent short
sides, pulling the fabric taut but keeping the
threads square to the frame.

5 Next, working on the other long side, pull the base fabric square to the edge of the frame and fix the third edge, paying particular attention to the corners. Finally, fix the fourth side in a similar way.

It is essential that the fabric is as taut as possible before you start to hook. If, when you have stapled the last edge, there are some ripples in the fabric, pull out some of the staples and refix the fabric so that it is smooth all across the surface.

6 Mark the borders of the rug on to the base fabric. Remember, you cannot hook right up to the edge of the frame, so draw the border about 12mm (^{1}/$_2$in) in from the inside edge of the frame. Place a sharp, soft pencil between two threads of the fabric and firmly pull it down towards you. Do not worry if the pencil line is not exactly square to the frame – if you have kept the pencil between the same two threads then the border will be square on all four corners.

7 Mark the centre of your rug by measuring halfway between the drawn edges, and then run a pencil line down and across the base fabric. This stage is not essential for this particular design but centre markings are often helpful as a guide.

Drawing the design

Using the pencilled shapes as a guide, draw the jigsaw design on to the base fabric with a waterproof felt-tipped pen (other types of marker could run when you wash or dry clean a rug).

You do not have to be too fussy with this design, but try to make the pattern fully interlocking and to keep the rows and columns square to each other.

Drawing out the design

Cutting strips of material

Cut some of your chosen materials into strips about 6 to 10mm ($\frac{1}{4}$ to $\frac{3}{8}$in) wide, always cutting on the straight of the material, never on the bias. Use either scissors or a rotary cutter and mat. Do not cut out a mass of strips at one time – after all, you may find that when you come to use the material you do not like the effect. The length of your material can be from 150mm (6in) upwards. (I usually keep a small frame nearby which I use to try out the effects of different materials.)

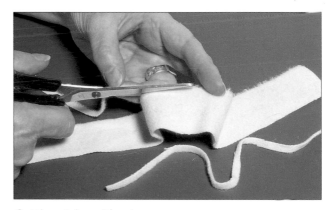

Cutting strips with scissors

If you use a rotary cutter and mat, ensure you have a straight edge of fabric. Lay this edge along one of the lines on the mat. Depending on the thickness of the material, you can sometimes double the fabric over. Place a metal-edged ruler the required distance from the edge and push the rotary cutter away from you in a firm, smooth movement.

Remember that rotary cutters are very sharp – never leave them unprotected, even for a moment. Get into the habit of releasing the blade into the safety guard as soon as you finish using the cutter.

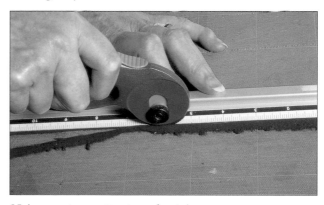

Using a rotary cutter to make strips

Starting to hook

1 You are now ready to begin, but first get used to handling the hook. Hold the hook in your hand as if you were going to write a letter, keeping the acute angle of the hook upwards as shown in the photograph. I am right-handed, so I hold the hook in my right hand and the strip of material in my left hand. If you are left-handed, reverse the following instructions.

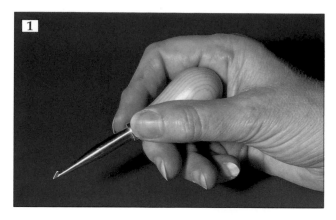

2 Holding the hook slightly at an angle, push it firmly through the base fabric from the design side to the back. Do not be too genteel – the bigger the hole the easier it is to bring the material back through. If you do not make a big enough hole the hook can catch on the threads when you bring back the hook.

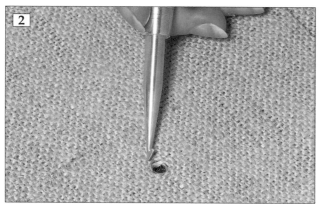

3 Do not worry about a hole being too big. When you make the next hole the threads displaced by the first one will close up automatically. It is this action that holds the looped strips of material firmly in the fabric.

4 Hold the strip of the material you are going to use loosely between the thumb and forefinger of your left hand. Never hold the strip tightly – always let it run freely through your fingers. Now position the strip under the framed fabric at the point where your hook will enter. Push the hook through the fabric from the design side and catch a loop of material in the hook.

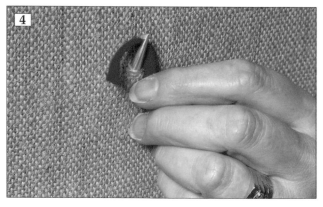

5 Pull the hook and the strip back up to the front of the work. Draw the loop up until you find a loose end and then leave it about 25mm (1in) above the surface. If you have pulled through a lot of the strip, just pull it back gently until just 25mm (1in) of it is sticking up above the fabric.

6 Working from right to left, move about two threads away and push your hook firmly into the fabric again. Holding the strip of material loosely between thumb and forefinger of the left hand and just above where the hook will be pushed in, engage the hook under the material and pull through a loop to the front, to a height of about 12mm (½in). Then disengage the hook.

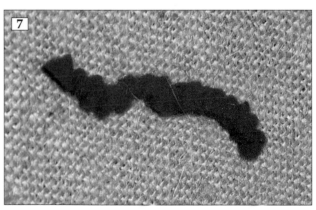

7 Work across the fabric, repeating the 'hook in, scoop and loop' movement. Unless you want a definitive straight line it is better to work in slight curves. This will let the loops meld better into each other.

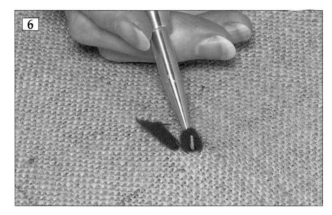

8 Turn the frame over and check the back of the fabric. You will know if you are making the loops correctly if you have what appears to be a row of running stitches on the back of the work. If there are lumps at the back, you are not making the holes big enough for the material to pass through easily.

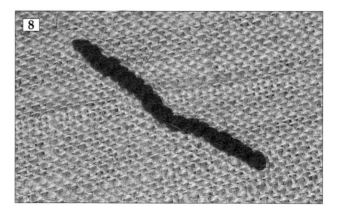

9 If you find you are pulling out the previous loop, you are not letting the strip run loosely between your thumb and forefinger. You are holding it too tight!

10 When you come to the end of the strip of material, pull its end up to the front of the fabric. Never leave any ends dangling at the back, nor be tempted to run a strip from one area to another. It is so easy to clip off your material and start again. If you do carry the material from one area to another, your hook could catch in the strip.

11 When you have finished one strip of material and you have brought its end up to the front, go back into the same hole and bring up the loose end of the next strip. This gives a double thickness of material – the same as with a loop. The loose ends can be trimmed level with the loops when the job is finished. However, do not worry if you cannot make joins in this way; it is not always possible.

When starting another row of loops, above or below the first row, always leave a gap of about two threads before making the first hole.

Hooking the design

1 Most experts say you should start in the centre of your work and move out, but I use my hook like a paintbrush and go where the fancy takes me. However, this design has to be outlined before the enclosed areas are filled in. When outlining with a single line I pull up the loops slightly higher than the rest of the work to ensure that the outlining does not get lost in the main mass of the work.

2 When you have completed the outlines, start to fill in the individual areas. Leave about two threads between each row of hooking. You can work above or below the line you have just hooked. If using wide strips, leave a few more threads between the loops and rows. The ideal is to have your loops close enough so that you do not see any base fabric, but not so tightly packed that they make the fabric 'hump'.

3 Continue hooking the design – either use up all of one material, spreading the colour around the rug, or work from the centre outwards.

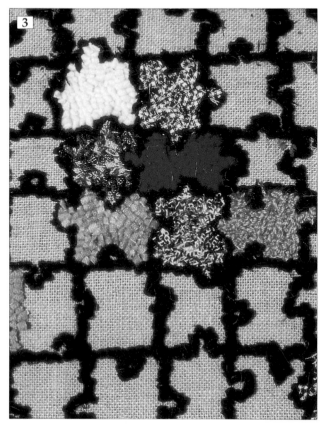

Tip
If I have a piece of work that has a lot of background, I do some of the pattern and some of the background – that way I do not leave all the background to be hooked at the end!

4 Continue hooking lengths of material until the rug is completed. However, before removing it from the frame, turn it over and check the back of the base fabric for gaps in the material. You will be surprised – although the front may appear quite solid, there will most probably be some gaps visible on the back. If there are any gaps, mark them by pushing wooden toothpicks into the gaps.

5 Turn the rug over and hook into the gaps marked with the toothpicks, trying not to pack the loops too tightly.

6 When you are happy with the hooking, trim off all the loose ends of material level with the tops of the loops.

7 Once the rug is finished, remove it from the frame. A proper staple remover is best for taking out the staples. You can use the head of a screwdriver, but take care not to damage the base fabric or your fingers.

8 Brush lightly over the pile with a firm clothes brush to remove any excess fluff.

9 Press the rug by laying it, pile side down, on to a large towel or blanket. Take a damp cloth and place it over the reverse of the rug. Press firmly with a hot iron, using a stamping rather than a gliding motion. Let the rug lie flat until dry.

Binding the rug

1 If necessary, cut down the base fabric to give a border of about 50mm (2in) all round the rug. Then make a diagonal cut across the corners to reduce the bulk when you finally hem the rug.

2 Using a strong thread, backstitch the binding as close against the last row of hooking as you can. I find I can get nearer by hand sewing but others may prefer to use a sewing machine and zipper foot. Always start halfway along one side, never at the corner. When going round the corners, ease the binding slightly to allow for mitring when you hem it down. Finally, turn back the two raw ends, butt them together and then join them neatly.

3 When you have finished sewing the binding, turn it back over the base fabric and hem it down, catching the stitches to the reverse of the rug. When you get to the corners, form the braid into a mitre by taking in the fullness, and catch it down. You can, if you wish, then sew over the mitred corner. If you have any spare strips of the materials you have used in making the rug, put a few of them between the rug and binding so that you have some easily accessible strips for repairs if necessary.

Tip
When binding an oval or round rug (see page 39), make small slashes in the excess base fabric round the rug. This ensures that when you turn the binding back to the wrong side the little sections of base fabric will overlap each other smoothly and prevent a bulky appearance. You may find that you have to ease the binding slightly as you go round.

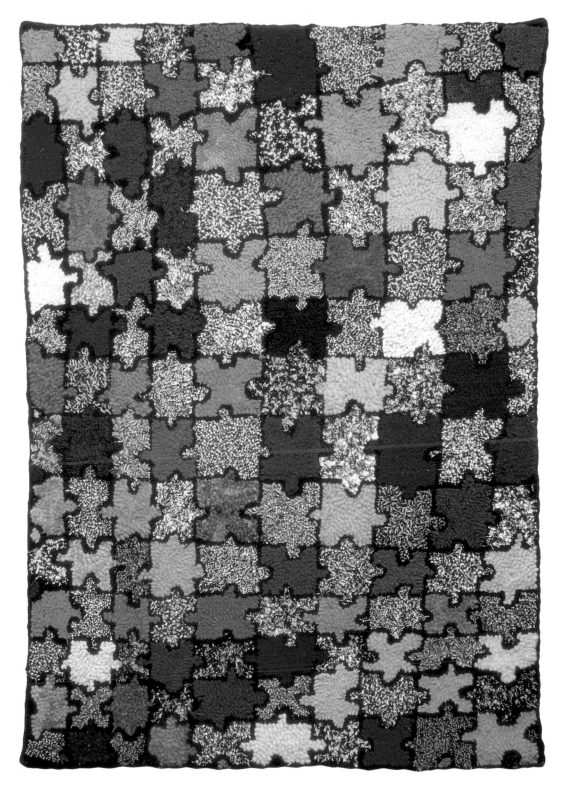

4 When you have completed sewing and hemming the binding, press the whole piece again on the reverse, so that the binding lies flat against the rug. Let the rug dry flat.

Design

Designs can be as complicated or as simple as you wish. I prefer simple designs but it is a matter of personal preference.

When considering designs, always bear in mind where the rug will be used. For example, if it is for the front of a fire, it will only be viewed from one direction. If it is for the centre of a room you must be able to view the design from all sides.

In this book I have tended to keep to simple designs which can be put into any setting. The design for the jigsaw rug (see pages 12–23) was drawn freehand, copying a few a shapes in various sizes. Similarly, for the heathery random rug on pages 28–29, I just drew a few guidelines on the rug, radiating out from the centre.

Designer aids

Nowadays, you do not have to be the world's greatest artist to produce pleasing designs. Stencils, French curves, protractors, patchwork templates, etc., can be used to help you create many different pictures and patterns.

Do not be afraid to try out your ideas. Take individual motifs from a stencil, or draw your own designs on pieces of cardboard, and play around with them until you get a pleasing effect.

Stylising a design.

Get inspiration from books, magazines, postcards, and stylise a picture into a simple line drawing.

Do not worry too much about detail; the drawn design is there for reference only. While you are hooking the rug, you can always decide to change certain areas – the markings will be covered by your hooked loops, so no one will ever know!

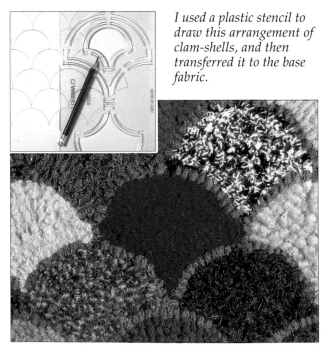

I used a plastic stencil to draw this arrangement of clam-shells, and then transferred it to the base fabric.

Obtain an enlarged photocopy from a picture and then trace the basic outlines of the picture. You can then enlarge the drawn design on to the base fabric.

Enlarging a design

When you have chosen a design, enlarge it to the size of your rug. You could go to a photocopying shop and get it enlarged to the required size. However, the process is not cheap and, sometimes, it can distort the design.

Alternatively, you can use the grid method to make a full-size pattern on a large sheet of graph paper or brown paper.

First, draw a grid over your original design – if you do not want to deface the original, fix a sheet of clear acetate or tracing paper over it and draw the grid on to that surface. The grid should have even-sized squares.

Now, draw a larger version of the grid on to another piece of paper, the same size as your rug. Then, in each of the large squares, draw what you see on the matching square of the small grid.

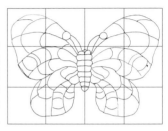

If you are not happy with your freehand drawing, use the grid method of enlargement to make a full-size pattern to trace from.

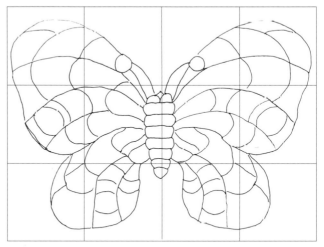

Transferring the design

Draw simple abstract designs, freehand, straight on to the fabric. If you are confident of your drawing skills, you can use the grid method of enlargement to draw the design straight on to the base fabric. Draw the enlarged grid on to the fabric by running a pencil firmly down between two channels of the thread (see page 14). Then, using a waterproof felt-tipped pen, transfer what you see on the smaller grid to the larger one on the fabric.

Alternatively, use a transfer pen and transfer paper to make a tracing of the full-size paper pattern. Lay the tracing face down over the base fabric and rub over the image with your fingernail, or a blunt instrument, to transfer the lines. If the transferred image is rather faint, go over the lines with a waterproof felt-tipped pen. When using transfer paper, remember that the transferred image is the reverse of the original.

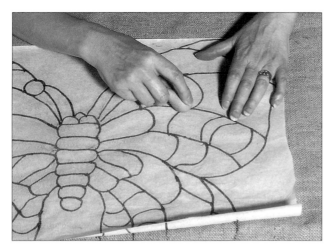

Use a transfer pen and paper to copy the design and a blunt instrument to rub the image on to the base fabric.

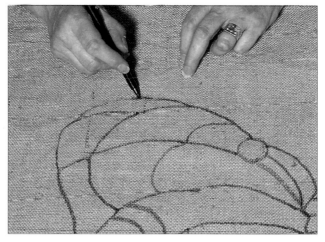

If the transferred image is rather faint, go over the lines with a waterproof felt-tipped pen.

Dyeing

This subject really calls for a book of its own, but I enjoy dyeing and overdyeing materials, especially as I like to use old materials, so I am including simple instructions in this book.

Dyes can add a new dimension to your rug making. You can create your own range of coloured fabrics by dyeing white or pale-coloured fabrics. With the exception of onion skins, which give a range of yellows and browns, I do not use many natural dyes, mainly because the process takes too long. I use synthetic dyes which are available in powder form.

I often use my microwave oven for dyeing woollen materials. You can only dye about 225g (8oz) dry weight of fabric, but it is quick and easy.

Mix 50ml (2fl.oz) of white vinegar and two drops of washing-up liquid in 1 litre (2pints) of warm water. Soak the fabric for about 1 hour and then gently squeeze out the excess water – it needs to be wet, but not dripping, so do not wring it out.

Cover your work surface with newspaper and a large sheet of plastic. Spread a piece of food-quality, plastic interleaving tissue (twice as wide as the piece of fabric and slightly longer) over the plastic (microwave cling-type film is not suitable). Place the wetted fabric flat in the middle of the interleaving tissue. Using gloved fingers, or a wallpaper seaming roller, work the dye right through the fabric. Random dyeing using different colours/shades can be quite effective. When you have finished dyeing, loosely fold the interleaving tissue to cover the fabric.

Pour 5mm (¼in) water into a microwave dish (keep one exclusively for dyeing), then fold the interleaving tissue parcel to fit the dish, and place the dish into the microwave. For a 650W machine, 'cook' the package for 7–10 minutes on a high setting, followed by 5–6 minutes on medium. If you have a thermometer, place it in the centre of the fabric at the end of the first period – the reading should be 80–85°C (170–180°F). If necessary, cook for a few more minutes on high before changing to

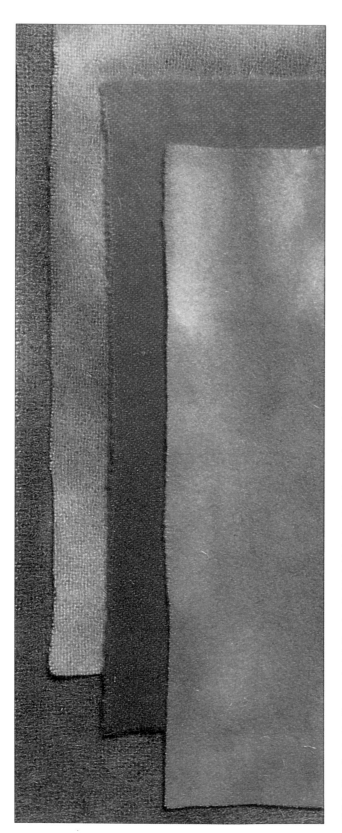

Produce your own range of colours by dyeing white or pale-coloured fabrics.

26

medium. Let the package cool thoroughly; rinse the fabric in tepid water and hang it up to dry.

Clean the inside of the microwave with soapy water when you have finished dyeing.

If you do not have a microwave, you can get the same results by steaming the package in a metal colander or steamer over a pan of water. Cover the top with a lid. Steam for about 15 minutes, allow to cool then rinse and dry the fabric.

Progressive shades of a colour can be obtained by multiple dipping.

Try overdying tweed/check materials. Here are four fabrics which have been overdyed with a violet dye.

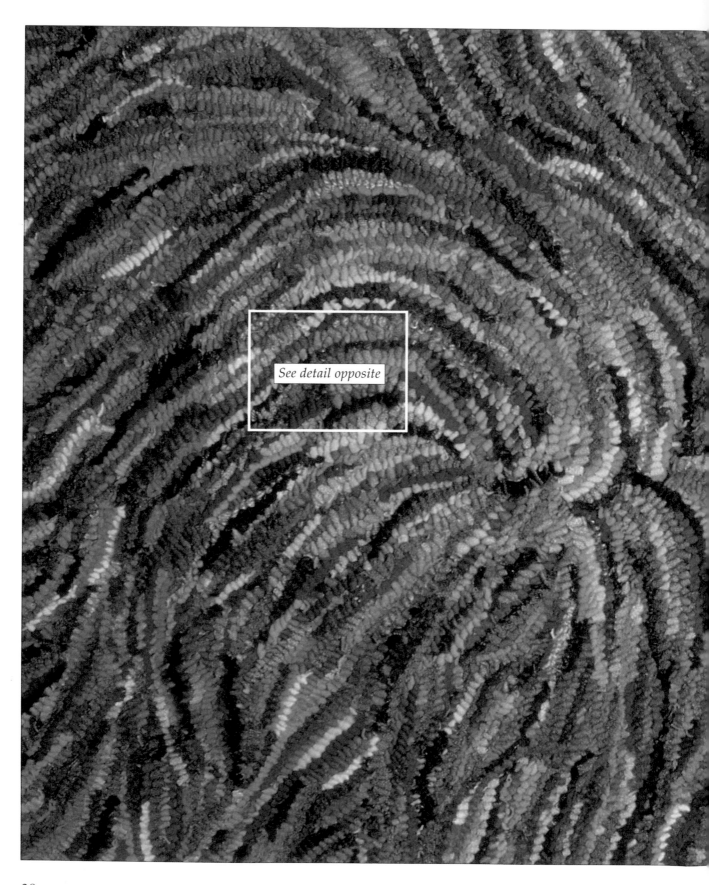

See detail opposite

Projects

Although the most popular use for rags is making rugs, a wide variety of other articles can be made. In this section I show you two rugs, a wall-hanging, a mirror surround, an unusual-shaped cushion, the seat and back of a director's chair and a seat pad. I have also seen hooking used for carpet bags, waistcoats, door stops, Christmas-tree ornaments, and ornamental fire screens. Some items are hooked finer than others – it just depends on the scale and the effect you want to achieve.

Random rug

This was a commission. The client wanted a random heathery design but, as she was not sure where she was going to put it, she required a design which would look pleasing whichever way you looked at it. I framed it up and marked out the edges and centre. Then, slightly off centre, I drew a few random curved lines radiating out. This was my only guide. I used a variety of fabrics – woollens, tweeds, worsted, and synthetics (all of a similar weight), and built up the colourways as I went, using the materials as a palette. Some fabrics were hand-dyed pieces, but I did not do any special dyeing for this project. The completed rug measures 610 x 810mm (24 x 32in).

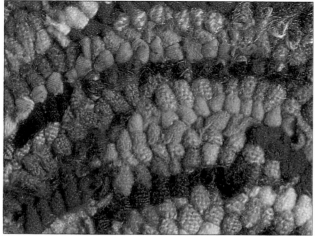

Detail taken from the completed random rug.

Cockerel wallhanging

This piece is based on a Chinese paper-cut, and was designed for me by a friend of many years, Roma Kirke. I wanted to get away from the conventional rectangular shape and the bottom of this was ideal.

Every part of the hanging was made from old blankets in their original colours. The border, the backing and the hanging tabs were made from a beautiful checked, woollen blanket; the hooked strips were cut from woollen and wool-mixture blankets. I used hessian (burlap) for the base fabric.

The design was long and thin, so I was able to work it on a frame without moving it about. I worked the piece as a rectangle, and cut the pointed bottom end when the hanging was bound.

When I had finished hooking I removed the work from the frame and trimmed off the excess base fabric, leaving 40mm (1½in) round all the edges. I pressed the work face down and then turned the three straight edges on to the back of the work, pressing them and tacking them down.

I laid the finished work, right side down, on to the backing fabric, and marked around the outside edges of the design with white chalk, allowing 10mm (½in) all round to cover the edges of the base fabric. Then, turning the two pieces and placing wrong sides together, I tacked (basted) the back to the front, from the centre of the work, taking long tacking stitches out to the sides.

Still keeping the work flat, I oversewed down the two long edges, ensuring that the hessian was not showing. I stopped just short of the shaped bottom. It is important to keep the hanging flat on the table as you work – it is like lining curtains – if you are not careful you finish up with a slightly raised curve.

I had a problem when it came to shaping the point at the bottom edge. Although I had cut slits into the excess base fabric to help form the curves, I found they would not lie flat, so I broke the habit of a lifetime and used white glue to get a good point. I cut the base fabric back to 10mm (½in) and stuck down the flaps of it with white glue. I spread the backing blanket down on to the glued area,

put a weight on top of the point to make it stay flat and left it there for several hours. When it was dry, I finished oversewing the backing fabric around the shaped edge. If you use this method, do not use too much glue or it will soak through the fabric and the weight will stick to your work.

The hanging tabs were attached in the same way. The material was non-fraying so I cut out the tabs, folded them over and spread glue over the bottom edges. I inserted each tab between the base fabric and the backing fabric. When the glue was dry, I stitched them to the backing, oversewing along the top edge, securing the back to the front. Finally, I removed the tacking (basting) stitches.

The hanging measures 580 x 900mm (23 x 35in).

Enlarge this pattern and make a hanging in your own range of colours.

Mirror surround

For this project, I decided first on the size of the frame in which the work was to be mounted. I marked these dimensions on to my base fabric – I used hessian (burlap) for this project. Using the transfer-pen method (see page 25), I marked out the design, adding about 60mm (2½in) all round, and then cut it out.

Once the base fabric was framed, I marked the centre of the work, then added lines to show the position of the mirror, making sure that the sides were square. As the design was quite small, I decided to work with narrow 6mm (¼in) strips, to bring up the detail. This meant that I had to work only with non-fraying woollen fabrics.

I used a special metallic material to add a touch of glitter around the flowers. When thinly cut and hooked, a pleasant iridescent effect is achieved. For articles such as wallhangings, this mirror surround, evening bags, etc., it produces an unusual effect and it is easy to use.

When I had finished the hooking, I removed the work from the frame and cut out the design, including the 60mm (2½in) border. I pressed it in the usual way then measured the hooked area accurately, and cut a piece of hardboard to this size. I also bought a mirror, the same size as the unhooked area.

I placed the worked piece right side down, flat on a table, and placed the hardboard on top. To remove excess bulk, I cut across the corners of the base fabric to within 20mm (¾in) of the design. I turned under 20mm (¾in) of the base fabric on all sides and, using a long length of very strong thread and a darning needle with a big eye, I laced the thread across the back, horizontally and vertically, pulling it taut and ensuring that the corners were turned in. If you do not turn the base fabric under to form a hem, it will fray and come away. When knotting additional lengths on to the threads, keep the knots in the centre of the work.

When I had finished lacing the back, I went over the threads, pulling them with my fingers to make them as tight possible, so that the front was completely taut. The hooking must be pulled right up to the edge of the hardboard. You will now see why I have told you to tie the knots in the centre of the work.

When the lacing was complete, I sewed the end of the thread into the base fabric and cut it off.

I used white glue (PVA) to fix the mirror on to the centre of the work, taking care not to get any glue on the hooked materials. I put some glue into the centre of the unhooked area; using a plastic knife, I carefully spread it out to the hooked edges.

Handling the glass mirror carefully, so as not to cut myself, I placed it firmly on to the glue. I put a soft cloth over the mirror, placed a heavy weight gently on top and left it until the glue was dry.

I then took the finished mirror surround to a picture framer to have it framed. If you do not want to go to this expense, you could sew an attractive fabric on to the back of the work to hide the lacings, and then fix hooks through the backing and the board.

The pattern for this mirror surround was designed by Roma Kirke. The finished piece measures 430 x 485mm (17 x 19in), with a 210mm (8¼in) square mirror tile mounted in the centre.

Butterfly cushion

I like to get away from conventional shapes. Here is an unusual shape for a neck cushion. Using a transfer pen and paper, I copied the design on to the base fabric (see page 25), and then framed it up. The materials I used included metallic fabric, jersey velvet, panné velvet and stretch fabric. I hooked all the outlines (the drawn lines on the pattern) slightly higher than the rest of the fabrics, to keep the looped lines visible.

When I had completed the hooking, I removed the work from the frame and trimmed the base fabric 25mm (1in) round the edge. I used a non-fraying velvet-like material for the backing, which I cut to the outline shape of the hooked butterfly, including the extra 25mm (1in). I placed the two sides of the butterfly together, right sides facing, and machine-hemmed around the edge, keeping as close as possible to the hooking, and leaving 75mm (3in) open. I turned the cushion right side out and filled it with fireproof stuffing, making sure that it bowed out the wings of the butterfly. I then carefully finished the hem by hand.

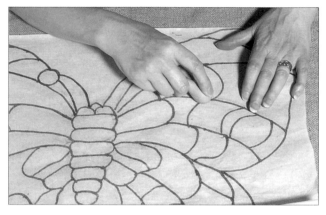

Use the handle of the hook to rub the design from the transfer paper on to the base fabric.

Enlarge this pattern and use it to make your own cushion. The wingspan of the butterfly opposite is 610mm (24in).

Director's chair

This chair was an inexpensive purchase. As the design on the seat and backrest was somewhat bland, I decided to create my own.

I measured both pieces and set up two frames, allowing at least another 25mm (1in) all around to allow for any take-up in the hooking.

I developed the design from two stencils, and then traced around them with a black waterproof pen. The stencils did not have any veining in the leaves, so I sketched them freehand. The materials were hand-dyed wool flannel for the leaves and a coloured blanket for the background. After completing both back and front, I removed them from their frames, turned 20mm (³/₄in) of excess base fabric on to the back of each and pressed them firmly. I then stitched the hooked seat design directly on to the original canvas chair, ensuring that they were both sewn tightly together. I felt that by stitching the design on to the chair in this way it would make the seat stronger and longer-lasting.

I worked in the same way with the chair back, making sure that the hooking was secured around the sides of the canvas.

Seat pad

I bought a seat pad from the local market, made a paper pattern of the slightly rounded shape, and folded it into four, vertically and horizontally, to find the centre. Using this pattern as a template, I measured the area, framed up the base fabric and then pinned the paper shape on to it, allowing 12mmm (1/2in) extra all round for the take-up of the hooking.

I marked the centre of the working area using a felt-tipped pen. I made a hole in the paper pattern, with the pen where the folds met, pushing it gently on to the base fabric. I was then able to match the centre of the stencil design to the centre of the pad. After working the pattern, I took it off the frame and applied the worked piece on to the pad, ensuring that any excess base fabric was tucked neatly under. By doing this I gave extra thickness to the seat pad.

Gallery

On these pages I have included a selection of rugs, pictures and wallhangings and I hope they will inspire you to greater accomplishments. Do not be afraid to experiment with designs, with different shapes and with the multitude of fabrics and materials around you.

SOLDIER
Designed by Ann Davies

Inspired by an old London transport poster, this rug is made from one hundred percent woollen materials.
Size: 485 x 860mm (19 x 34in)

OPTICAL ILLUSION
Designed by Ann Davies

A geometric circular design with an entwined pattern. I wanted to get away from conventional rug shapes, so I decided to emphasize the shapes in the design by making points around the edge.

The fabrics used include tweeds, cotton velvet and a pink blanket.
Size: 700mm (27^{1}/$_{2}$in) diameter

RADIATING SQUARES
Designed by Ann Davies

A geometric oval design with short straight edges around the circumference. It is made with woollen fabrics that include a lot of tweeds.
Size: 720 x 625mm (28 x 25in)

39

40

DES-RES

Designed by Roma Kirke

A traditional English cottage worked in woollen materials. The thatched roof is camel-hair coating, the house and garden are worked in tweeds and other woollen fabrics.
Size: 600 x 885mm (24 x 35in)

ART DECO
Designed by Ann Davies (inspired by the designs of Charles Rennie Mackintosh)
The fabrics are woollen and include tweeds and a hand-dyed pink blanket.
Size: 570 x 810mm (22^1/$_2$ x 32in)

SEA CREATURES
Designed by Roma Kirke

This circular rug lends itself well to the movement of the sea urchins. The background is green woollen tweed with specks of black. The other materials are also woollen.
Size: 710mm (28in) diameter

44

Right

AUTUMN LANDSCAPE

Designed by Ann Davies

This landscape was inspired by the view from an aeroplane. The fields are made from a number of different weaving yarns and fine cut materials, and the cornfields are embroidered with a long and short stitch. Some of the fields are worked in reverse hooking: they are hooked from the back so that the front shows the broad running stitches (see page 17).

Size: 320 x 530mm (12$\frac{1}{2}$ x 21in)

Opposite

LANDSCAPE

Designed by Ann Davies

The landscape is a source of perennial inspiration; it never ceases to provide ways for the artist or craftsperson to interprate its beauty. I chose to make this design into a wallhanging so that I could use a wide variety of fabrics. They include tweeds, multi-coloured velvets, worsted, unspun tops and viscose.

Size: 610 x 810mm (24 x 32in)

Cleaning and storing

Cleaning

Clean lightly soiled rugs by gently sweeping a soft brush over the surface – or use a vaccuum cleaner. If I use my machine I place a piece of net over the cleaning nozzle and use a low setting so that the fabric pieces are not disturbed.

Soiled rugs should not be washed unless they are heavily marked. Remove any marks as soon as they are made. If the rug becomes heavily marked and you wish to wash it, use a gentle proprietary foam rug cleanser. Make sure the colours will not run or bleed by first testing a small piece on the reverse side. Dab the foam on to the surface of the rug, and remove any marks with a clean cloth. If the rug is badly soiled, or if you are worried about the cleaning process, you can always have it dry cleaned.

Frequent washing will cause hessian (burlap) to deteriorate, so be careful when selecting your base fabric. If you want to make a rug for an area that will be in constant use, choose a stronger fabric, such as linen. If you care for your rugs in the right way, they should last for a long time.

Storing

Storing materials can be a problem, especially if you are an inveterate horder like me. Ideally they should be sorted into colours and the different types of fabric. I have found the best method is to store all the materials in large, clear plastic sacks so that you can see what you have collected, Sometimes it is not easy to be that organised!

Wash the fabrics before putting them into the plastic bags. This will help to deter moths. Sprays can be used, but they sometimes have a distinctive odour, so make sure they are used in well ventilated rooms, or outside in the fresh air.

Finished rugs and wallhangings should be carefully stored in cotton bags. Check they are moth-free before they are packed. If they have to be stored in plastic bags, make sure it is not for any length of time, or they will start to deteriorate. If you have to carry the finished pieces, never fold them. Always roll them up with the loops on the outside.

Opposite
BRING ON THE CLOWN
Designed by Roma Kirke

This design is ideal as a rug or wallhanging for a child's room. Woollen materials make up most of the hooked area. A multi-check fabric was used for the trousers. I also used stretch metallic fabric to add glitter to the hat, ruff and waistcoat, and some camel-hair coating on the background.

Size: 540 x 735mm (21¹/₄ x 29in)

Index